Tending Fences

Tending Fences:

BUILDING SAFE AND HEALTHY RELATIONSHIP BOUNDARIES

The Parables of Avery Soul

TERRY BARNETT-MARTIN

ILLUSTRATED BY SUSAN EBERHARDT

TRUE PURPOSE PUBLISHING

Tending Fences: Building Safe and Healthy Relationship Boundaries; The Parable of Avery Soul

For information about this title or to order other books and/or electronic media, contact the publisher:

True Purpose Publishing
9891 Irvine Center Drive #200
Irvine, CA 92618
www.truepurposepublishing.com
truepurposecoach@cox.net

ISBNs:
Soft bound: 978-0-9910727-6-7
Hard bound: 978-0-9910727-4-3
Ebook: 978-0-9910727-7-4

Printed in the United States of America

Cover and interior design: 1106 Design

Self-Help/Inspirational/ Boundaries in Relationships.

To Joe and Tim,
I love you more than words can say.
I am grateful beyond measure
for all that you give me,
for the way that you love,
and for all that you teach me.

■ ■ ■

Thanks and Love
All Around

I am so thankful to the team of supportive and creative wonders who helped me to get this book finished and polished. To Sue Eberhardt, for your adorable and charming illustrations that brought this book to life, and for your keen eye and expert editing. To Therese Barnett, for your patient proofreading and unending encouragement. To Maureen Foerster, for your detailed and painstaking final edit. Because of all of you this book lives and breathes better. To Phyllis Barnett for your generous words of enthusiasm and encouragement for *Tending Fences*. It has meant so much to me along the way. A special thanks to Diane White for helping me to properly format the illustrations when I was lost in the maze of technology. I am eternally grateful for everyone who helped me along the way. My love to you all.

■ ■ ■

Table of Contents

Anita Messenger helps Avery Soul tremendously by
referring him to Theo Sage when his roof and ranch
house are in desperate need of repair. Theo Sage is
a master carpenter who is always on call and seems
to show up just when Avery needs him. He is kind
and patient, and possesses unending wisdom which
he imparts when asked.

Gabianne Bossi is a nosy, meddlesome neighbor who
believes that the world should revolve around her. In
her quest to control situations, she looks for ways to
rile people up and get them on her side. She is the
master of the mob mentality maneuver and can stir
up a crowd with a few well placed rumors.

The Dearones are Avery's neighbors whom he loves
as if they were his own family. When tragedy befalls
them, he feels as if it happened to him too.

Angel Goodheart is a dear friend of Avery's and one for whom he feels protective. Avery finds that his misguided good intentions make Angel feel small and inept.

Skip Owt and Sissy Neaner are neighbors around whom Avery feels invisible.

Myne Memine is in the habit of taking whatever he wants when he wants it. He makes the mistake of doing that with Avery and loses a good opportunity. Tru Onner, a neighbor of Avery's with steadfast integrity and respect for himself and others, does the right thing and benefits greatly.

Alvin Schemer is a neighbor who constantly uses the 'divide and conquer' game plan to gain control with a group of Avery's friends. Timmy Trueblue and Sam Noble are close friends of Avery's who fall prey to Alvin Schemers manipulations.

Mo Betta is a friend of Avery's who understands the need for fences and shares a great story with him about how giving from anything but a pure heart is not truly giving at all.

Al and Alice Consuming are good neighbors but their overflowing ivy gets out of hand and compromises Avery's ranch.

Introduction:
A Word about Fences

A FENCE IS DEFINED as a "barrier that encloses," with synonyms that include: to protect, fortify, and secure. Fences also represent connectors that provide healthy conjunctions and most importantly, a sense of security. Built with self-respect and regard for self and others, fences are the cornerstones to healthy relationships and deep peace of mind.

Acting as barriers and dividers, fences can both shore things up and hold things in. They mark property lines so people can clearly see what is or is not theirs. Fences can connect one side to the other or protect one side from the other. They are there to filter, contain, and promote respect. It is up to each of us to decide what kind of fence is right for each relationship in our lives. For instance, with someone you love and trust deeply your fence will be clear and accessible. It will be a fence on which both of you can gently lean, comforted by the knowledge that you are safe and that neither will intrude upon the other. Conversely, with someone who invades your life, imposing on and disrespecting your thoughts and beliefs, a tall, fortified and almost impenetrable fence is in order. Likewise, if you find yourself easily infringing upon another, it is important that you exemplify your respect for them by building a proper fence to contain yourself.

Tending Fences is a collection of stories about a man named Avery Soul. He lives on an expansive ranch for which he is completely responsible. His life is dedicated to developing the potential of his land, and he is always in the process of fixing or remodeling his ranch house, which stands in the front acre of his vast property just off the neighborhood road. A creative, resourceful, and respectful person, Avery works hard to be the best he can be. His projects to plant, fix, or remodel his ranch are really work he is doing to improve himself.

Avery Soul is every person, every soul. He is me. He is you. The ranch, the ranch house and Avery's neighbors are metaphors for life. The ranch represents Avery's self, including his potential for growth and experience. The ranch house is his mind and heart. It contains his dreams, ideas, thoughts and perspectives. It is where he lives and from which he gathers his strength and direction as he goes out into the world.

The neighbors represent the relationships in his life that pose a challenge in some way, causing him to use his ingenuity to build strong and healthy boundaries. The fences both protect Avery and connect him to his neighbors. They differ in materials and construction from neighbor to neighbor, depending on the nature of the relationship, and they provide a safe place for Avery's well-being and peace of mind.

The characters in these stories represent people whom we all have met, and may have been, in some way or another, during our lives. The stories illustrate universal dilemmas, and Avery tackles them with his well-considered solutions.

His simple act of building proper fences makes life better for both Avery and his neighbors. As the saying goes, "Good fences make good neighbors." (Frost)

These stories in *Tending Fences* help to unclutter, sort out, and set straight relationships in a simple yet profound way. Visualizing and building proper fences, whether literally or figuratively, helps to remedy difficult relationships in our lives, freeing us up to comfortably be and feel our best. ▪

The Roof

TORRENTS OF RAIN POURED DOWN on the tiny figure clinging to the roof of the ranch house. Avery Soul was being blown this way and that as he tried to put plastic sheets over the tile roof. Inside the house, pots, pans, and buckets of all sizes were positioned to catch the gushing streams of water pouring down from the high ceilings above. He couldn't stop the rain from falling, but he hoped he could stop it from destroying the inside of his ranch house.

It seemed fruitless until he heard a voice calling to him through the howling wind. It was Anita Messenger, his neighbor and friend, calling from across the fence and pleading with him to be careful. She had spotted him from the upstairs window of her three-story ranch house and immediately decided to see if she could help in some way. Braving the storm herself, she ran to grab her umbrella and raced to their adjoining fence to tell Avery about the most excellent roofer and master carpenter.

When he heard Anita calling to him, Avery turned and accidentally slid down the steep roof nearly falling off the side. Fortunately, he landed right near his ladder which he grabbed onto for dear life. He carefully climbed down the slippery steps and dashed across the yard to where Anita was holding an oversized umbrella to cover him. Handing him Theo Sage's business card, she yelled over the wind and rain, "He might even see you today to assess what needs to be done." He thanked her and then made a run for the ranch house. Once on his porch, he watched to make sure Anita made it safely back to her house as the wind whipped up and nearly turned her umbrella inside out. She waved to him when she reached her door and he breathed out, suddenly realizing he had been holding his breath.

The temporary fix of plastic sheeting on the roof helped a little, but Avery knew he was in trouble and needed the help of a professional roofer. He called Theo Sage, and within a few hours the roofer was at his front door. Theo knew a lot about structures, from the foundation to the roof and everything in between. After an extensive assessment he told Avery that although the water level outside was high and the house was slightly flooded, his foundation was solid. He continued on to say that once the roof was replaced, he

could begin to repair the inside of the house. When the rain finally subsided for a while, Theo began to work on the roof. Always curious, Avery asked if he could watch him work, and Theo invited him to assist instead. At first he showed Avery each step necessary to rebuild the roof, then he let him try. Before he knew it Avery had become quite skilled at fixing his own roof. Theo was pleased to have such a willing apprentice.

Once the roof was completed, though achy from the hard labor, Avery was proud of himself and felt safe in his home again. Inside the house, the floors and walls were badly warped and damaged so Theo showed him how to shore up the structure, install new walls, and repair the wood floors. After several weeks of meticulous work, the ranch house was stronger and more beautiful than ever. Avery had learned so much from Theo Sage, and he had a feeling that in the years to come he would learn even more. ▨

The "Change Your Garden" Campaign

I t was late Spring and Avery Soul's vegetable garden was flourishing as it dripped and flowed like a wild river over the ample ground in which it was planted. He had spent hours without end researching and developing his own unique design and methods for planting. He enriched the soil with the minerals and nutrients needed to grow healthy and nourishing vegetables. Because he did not want to use pesticides, he devised other ways to keep bugs, birds, and other critters from destroying his garden. He used pinwheels, chimes, a variety of scarecrows, windsocks, whirligigs, "good" insects, and insect repelling plants throughout the garden. Once the garden was all set up, it looked more like a circus than a garden. And Avery was pleased.

A few months earlier his neighbor from across the way, Gabianne Bossi, was perched up high on the hill of her side yard watching as Avery assembled his garden. She shook her head and tch tch tched, annoyed with his design. She spoke in a scolding shout. "This will not do! Gardens are supposed to be in straight, furrowed rows with clearly marked signs for each vegetable. You are doing it all wrong! It looks like a big mess. And since it faces my house and I have to look at it, I WANT YOU TO CHANGE IT!"

Avery, familiar with Gabianne Bossi's methods of force-fully getting her way, replied with a patient voice at first.

"Now, Gabi, this is my own design and it works for me." "Humph!" she snorted, as she turned to go complain to the other neighbors. She spoke to several people before the afternoon was over, many of whom had never met Avery Soul, nor had they ever seen his garden. She craftily enlisted them in her self-serving campaign to change his garden. She threatened him, stating that if he didn't change his garden to her specifications she would get even more people for her campaign. Avery didn't. And so she did.

Early one morning, when Avery went into town to buy some gardening supplies, he was stunned by the number of people, led by Gabianne Bossi, walking in a circle in front of the store, carrying picket signs reading, "Change Avery Soul's Garden," and chanting the same. He quickly ducked into the store to purchase what he needed. Once inside, the chanting faded, but a few people inquiring about the whole ordeal, approached him. Some suggested that it would be easier if Avery just changed his garden to please the picketers so they would stop harassing him. He didn't agree.

When Avery had finished his shopping he made his way through the picket line, which had moved to block the door of the gardening store. The chant, "CHANGE YOUR GARDEN! CHANGE YOUR GARDEN!" grew louder as Gabianne Bossi wound up the crowd as he tried to get to the parking lot. He looked around to find faces of people he had never met, mixed with people he had known his whole life. Gabi stood with her hand on her hip and a smug look of satisfaction on her face as she watched him wind through the picketing crowd. When Avery got to his truck he took one last glance and felt sick to his stomach with disappointment and anxiety. Once home he found more picketers forming a line at his front gate. He couldn't believe it. "Don't these people have anything better to do?" he grumbled out loud to himself. He quickly drove into his driveway, careful not to bump into the picketers who were attempting to stop him. He parked behind the ranch house and took refuge inside.

Later that morning when the 'Change Your Garden' campaign was in full swing, a number of supporters approached Theo Sage's doorstep where he sat lacing up his boots in preparation for his day's work. He listened carefully to what they had to say and asked them some questions. "If Avery Soul grows his vegetable garden and it looks like a circus, so what? How does that really affect you?" The small group of campaigners considered what he said and came back with a few "yeah, but" responses, but eventually walked away disgruntled with Theo's lack of support for their misguided cause.

Though happy with his garden design, Avery was troubled by the "Change YOUR Garden" chant he heard wherever he went. He had spent years perfecting his design with proven results, and it both hurt and angered him greatly that several people were now demanding that he change it to please them. Thanks to Gabianne Bossi, who scurried around town talking up her cause, Avery was feeling seriously outnumbered. He knew there were some neighbors and friends who appreciated his innovative method and could see the genius in it. But the number of campaigners was growing. Sad and lonely, Avery went for a walk to the far-reaching corners of his ranch to think. He noticed the rich, dark soil, the colorful flowers, and beautiful huge trees along his path. He surveyed his ranch that seemed to go on forever, and saw familiar land, which he had tilled and planted, and on which he had built shelter for himself and his loved ones. There was also, in the distance, land that he had yet to know and it was there that he was headed. He usually felt at home walking by himself on his ranch, but today he felt uncomfortable in his own company.

The day was crystal clear and sunny. The sun warmed him like a long lost friend as he walked a new path. He heard the "Ping, ping, smash" of a hammer in the distance, so he walked towards it. As he got closer he recognized Theo Sage, and for a while he watched him build a fence. They smiled at one another but said nothing. Theo kept a watchful eye on Avery and after some time he asked him, "Would you like to talk, Ave?" Avery looked up slowly, warmed by the familiar nickname Theo called him, and began to tell him the story of his garden and the 'Change YOUR Garden'

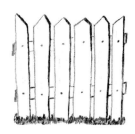

"Some people follow a map.
Others follow their heart.
Both are good."

campaign. After hearing the whole story, Theo was quiet for a while. Then he smiled kindly and said, "Ave, there are different kinds of people, each with his or her own picture of the way things should be. There are those who feel more comfortable with tried and true ways, straight lines and labels for everything. When harvest comes it is predictable and safe. And then there are those who are more comfortable trying new ways and experimenting. For these individuals the building, design and planting is more important, or at least as important, as the crops themselves. It is the ingenuity needed for the process that excites these people. In both ways of doing things there is certain order, but not the same kind. And they focus on different values.

One gardener values the way it looks with neat rows that are well marked and easily accountable. The other gardener revels in the process of creating a unique design experimenting with homemade soil enriching recipes, excited for the possibilities. Some people follow a map. Others follow their heart. Both are good."

Avery stood quietly for a while drinking in what Theo had said. Nodding his head slowly, then ever faster, he thanked him and bid him goodbye as he turned to begin his long hike back to the ranch house. As he walked he thought of a plan that would both please him and end the campaign. His pace quickened to a near run as he felt the relief of his new idea give him energy.

He gathered materials from all over his ranch to build a quaint picket fence around his garden. He toiled all day, every day, for a week—digging, cutting, building and painting—until the fence framed his garden high enough to ward

off the scrutiny of the campaigners, while it added a bit of charm to his design. He installed a round-topped gate on two sides of the garden fence for easy access, and he painted the whole fence with several coats of bright white paint. He hung perfectly tuned wind chimes from a few of the fence slats, and a hand-painted sign that read, "Avery Soul's Garden." When he was finished he truly liked it. He had kept his own design of the garden and framed it like a beautiful picture with the picket fence.

The campaigners quieted down and dispersed. Many felt foolish for their participation in Gabianne Bossi's cause, realizing they had been played in her game once again. They came to know Avery Soul better as the years went by and even began to employ some of his methods for their own gardens. ▪

The Dearone's Tragedy

A very Soul woke to the sound of sirens and the heavy, pungent smell of smoke. It seemed the sirens and the commotion stopped almost exactly at his house. He jumped up, startled by the thoughts that raced through his head . . . his family, his pets and animals, all his true treasures, Are they okay? Are they safe? Is the ranch house burning down? How would he get to them all and get them to safety?

As he ran through the house worrying and assessing, he gradually became aware that, in fact, it was not his home that was on fire. His loved ones were safely huddled together hugging each other and wondering what to do. He quickly pulled on a loose pair of overalls to cover his long johns and bolted out the front door to the Dearone's ranch. He had known Buddy and Ally since they were in high school, and they were like family to him. It was their ranch that was ablaze against the night sky. Smoke poured from a hole in the roof and through every window. People were frantically screaming, "Where are they? Did they get out?"

Buddy and Ally had three young kids, two dogs, and three cats that all lived in the house. Avery heard the two dogs barking near the back of the house, so he ran toward them and found the paramedics attending to Buddy and Ally and the kids. They were getting ready to transport them to the hospital. Avery could see the shock setting in

as their eyes began to glaze over, and a stunned look came over their faces like a dark cloud. Ally started to cry, caught somewhere between loss and gratitude. Her family was safe, for that she was deeply thankful. But their home, their photos, their irreplaceable treasures, their family heirlooms, and possibly their beloved pets, were gone . . . just gone. Loss and joy all in one moment, it was too overwhelming to comprehend. Buddy and the children were loaded into a large ambulance while Ally took a last look. Avery promised to take their two dogs home with him and to keep an eye out for the three cats they loved so much. The sirens wound up and got louder as the ambulance made its way through the crowd that had gathered.

Avery watched the flashing lights until they were out of sight, then gathered the two dogs and brought them to his

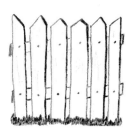

"In fact," Anita Messenger whispered,
"from my side of the fence, this is a miracle."

was not consumed with the tragedy, but rather she focused on the fact that she was safe, the Dearones were safe, and he and his loved ones were safe. "In fact," Anita Messenger whispered, "from my side of the fence this is a miracle."

Avery was quiet for a moment as he noticed that his muscles began to systematically relax. He slowly nodded as the grip of fear in his throat gave way to tears of relief. The heap of ashes and debris that was once the Dearones' home was a reminder that life is precious. And most important for him to remember, from his side of the fence, though it would be sadly different for a while, it was indeed a miracle that they all survived. ■

■ ■ ■

Dung Rain

On an unseasonably cold Spring morning, Avery Soul began to plant some new young trees along one of his fences. As he prepared the soil and dug a hole for a five foot tall Liquidambar, he pictured what they all would look like in ten years. He had already planted two Sugar Maples, and three Quaking Aspens. Several White Birch and Pepper trees were still waiting for their turn to be lifted into their own nests in the warmth of the earth. He had long needed shade on that side of the ranch that sweltered in the summer sun. As he dug a hole for each tree, he hummed lightly to himself. He had a tune in his head that seemed to come from nowhere and he couldn't shake it. By mid-morning the sun had come out and had begun to warm his achy, cold hands.

He was lifting a fragile, new White Birch into the hole he had prepared when out of the corner of his eye he saw something flying towards him. It landed squarely on his shoulder. In a flash he knew what it was because of its familiar stench. He quickly grabbed his hand trowel to scrape it off. Just as he got the bulk of it off another one came careening towards him. Suddenly cow dung was coming at him faster than he could duck and cover. He was splattered with it from his hat to his boots. A rancher all of his life, cow dung was nothing new to him, however, he was quite

disturbed that it was flying through the air in all directions. Once he found a safe place where the rain of dung could not reach him, he peered across the yard to discover its origin. He noticed the shiny end of a shovel catching the sunlight every couple of seconds. Then he saw the tip of a familiar ranch hat bobbing above the fence. It was his neighbor Bubba Bueser, generally an intensely angry and frustrated man, feverishly shoveling dung.

It was hard to move close enough to get his attention, so Avery called out from a distance. "Yo! Bub, you're flinging your dung over the fence into my yard!" He could see Bub arrogantly nodding as he continued to heave the dung over the fence. Avery tried several ways to get his attention to tell him to stop. Finally, Avery yelled angrily, "Bubba, stop using my ranch as your dumping ground!"

Even though he tried to reason with him, nothing seemed to work. Cow manure was flying all over the place, plopping on the ground, on the tender branches of the fragile new trees, in the flower beds, on pathways, and on the garden shed behind which Avery had taken cover.

He thought anxiously to himself, trying to come up with a solution for his dilemma, and then said out loud as if going into battle mode, "This calls for desperate measures!" He eyed a stack of freshly cut wood planks that he had intended for a patio cover. But this day it appeared that the wood had another purpose. The custom cut planks measured almost twenty feet long and there were enough of them to span the full length of the fence where the two ranches met. He buckled on his carpenter tool belt, filled it with a power hammer and a battery powered drill and screwdriver, and dashed to the pile of wood planks. Hoisting one plank at a time on to his shoulder he moved as quickly as he could through the

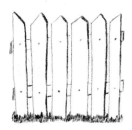

Finally, Avery yelled,
"Bubba, stop using my ranch
as your dumping ground!"

growing piles of manure and began to build a taller fence to stop the rain of dung. He left the original fence in place and added strength and height to it with each new plank. It was a messy job with the constant shower of dung, and it was hard to see what he was doing. His arms got so tired and spent from single-handedly wielding the twenty-footers from the side of the house to the fence. Time after time the dung hit a plank just as he was fastening it to the existing fence, knocking it momentarily out of place. It took all of his might to realign it and hold it in place while under siege. When he was about a quarter of the way through he saw someone waving to him from the front gate of his ranch. It was his treasured friend, Theo Sage, holding up his toolbox and motioning that he was willing to help if he needed him. Avery stood up for a moment to wave to Theo to come on over, and was immediately hit square in the middle of his chest with a plop of manure. Theo ran up, scraped the dung off Avery's chest, and then lifted the plank and steadied it while Avery fastened it into place. Once it was secured, Theo jogged over to get the next plank while Avery installed a few more screws to fortify the fence. They worked like a well-oiled machine for what seemed like hours. Avery was amazed at how Theo anticipated every step of the job and was so helpful. He was sure he wouldn't have been able to do it without him. As they neared the last few planks they could see much better and nodded to one another that it was good.

When the fence was finished Avery turned to thank Theo, and as he did he realized they had hardly said a word to each other during the siege. They just knew what

needed to be done and did it together. Theo gave Avery a big hug, manure and all, and they both chuckled. But as they turned to walk to the ranch house to wash up they found themselves shin deep in dung. At first Avery was disgusted and overwhelmed with the aftermath of the dung onslaught. He briefly fantasized about dumping all of it back into Bubba Bueser yard with his old front loader. Then Theo made a suggestion. "Ave, sometimes our greatest nemesis can show us what we most need in order to grow." After pondering for a moment, Avery looked at his new trees, some with dung hanging off of their branches and quickly decided what to do. As usual Theo stood ready to help and without a word they each took a shovel and began to turn the manure into the dirt, mixing it in to enrich the

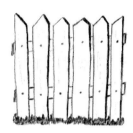

Avery was amazed at how Theo Sage had anitcipated every step of the job and was so helpful. He was sure he wouldn't have been able to accomplish it without him.

soil. They packed a concentration of the mixture around the base of each of the trees, knowing it would help them grow. Then they spread the rest of it over the side yard to help the grass grow. When they were done with the dung work they returned to the ranch house to clean up. Theo reminded Avery that he could call him anytime he needed him, then he bid him good day. As Avery watched him walk down the path to the gate, he felt so grateful that Theo Sage had shown up when he did.

After a warm, rejuvenating shower Avery put on a fresh set of clothes and relaxed with a lemonade on the front porch swing. He thought quietly to himself about the whole ordeal, but after a few minutes he found himself giggling, then laughing out loud at his mental picture of the dung flying through the air at him. He had been angry at first, and then a little scared wondering how to stop Bubba Bueser's "rain of terror." He thought of how ridiculous the whole thing was. The nerve of Bub to fling his dung over the fence was so audacious it was laughable. Even more than that, Avery was in awe of Theo's willingness to help no matter how hard the work. He sighed with great gratitude that Theo Sage definitely had his back, and that he was not alone. It made all the difference for him in his battle to save his ranch.

Avery was proud of himself for the quick action he took to save his little trees. And he was amazed at how he was able to use the dung to better his ranch. Though it was clearly not his dung in the first place, he had found good use for it by turning it into fertilizer for his own land's growth.

Then Theo made a suggestion...
"Ave, sometimes our greatest nemisis
can show us what we need most
in order to grow."

Even after it stood for many months, Bubba Buser continued to shovel manure, trying to clear the new fence. As he sat on his porch swing or worked in the side yard, Avery often heard the "chuff, chuff, plop" of the shovel and the dung as it hit the planks on Bub's side of the tall fence, and fell back to the ground with a thud. He pictured his troubled neighbor with dung hanging from his rancher hat and hoped that Bub would soon figure out a more productive way to deal with his own manure. Until then, the masterfully built fence would keep Avery and his ranch safe from any further dung rain. ▪

■ ■ ■

The Fire on the Other Side

I t was a beautiful day. The sky was a cloudless deep blue and the sun was comfortably warm. The air was perfect for a deep, refreshing breath. Avery Soul had been working in the pastures among his horses, making sure that they were healthy and eating well. Alone with his thoughts, he was thoroughly enjoying the early morning on his ranch.

As he worked, he began to smell smoke. At first, he thought nothing of it, but he scanned the horizon for clouds of smoke just the same. He saw only a small puff of smoke coming from the ranch of his good friend and neighbor, Ben Ther. Ben's land joined Avery's at the southwest corner of his ranch. Avery started to feel a little nervous as he saw the smoke puffs turn to billows. Instinctively, he ran to get the fire hose and he lugged it over and through the split rail fence that divided their land. He then attached it to the fire hydrant he had installed on his ranch, and he was ready to fight the blaze.

Avery could see Ben in the distance just standing and watching the fire ravaging one of his large fields. He was alone and Avery saw that he didn't seem to be taking any action to put the fire out, so he jumped the fence and began to spray down the flames. Because he was so focused on saving the field, he didn't notice Ben waving his arms or hear him yelling to stop.

After the fire was out Avery turned to look at Ben anticipating thanks for his heroic help. Instead, as Ben approached him, Avery could see by the look on his face that he was not at all pleased. Ben let him know that he had deliberately started the controlled burn to re-seed his field, and he had all of the tools and equipment to contain the fire. Avery had acted too quickly with no idea that Ben had the whole thing under control. He apologized profusely as he sheepishly gathered his gear and jumped back over the fence to his own ranch.

This was not the first time that Avery Soul had rushed into a situation without checking out what was really going on. But he swore to himself that it would be the last time he jumped over the fence uninvited. He knew well the value of a good fence and a good friendship.

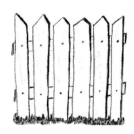

Avery swore to himself that it
would be the last time he jumped
over the fence uninvited. He knew the
value of a strong fence and a good friendship.

Later that week Avery noticed that Ben Ther was add-
ing some decorative wrought ironwork to the existing fence
between their ranches. Avery understood that Ben's fence
needed to be a little more difficult for him to jump over, giving Avery a chance to think before he jumped. He ambled
over to the fence to admire Ben's work, and they silently
nodded at each other and smiled. ■

Making Light

Avery Soul was taking a snooze on the sunny side of his porch, the spot where he felt most peaceful and safe. He had worked all morning tending to the spring flowers planted alongside the porch. They flourished in the full sun exposure that amply warmed them. Snap dragons, Verbena, Black-eyed Susan, Lavender, and Periwinkle were arranged in a beautiful pattern of color at varying heights filling the sumptuous planter, with White Alyssum framing Mother Nature's colorful party.

As he rested, soothed by the sun and his whole body comfortably supported in every way by the porch hammock, he thought how lucky he was to have this peaceful moment of bliss. He breathed it in, relaxing every muscle in his body and soon fell into a deep, restful sleep. His rest lasted only twenty minutes but felt like a full night's sleep. The chill of a sudden darkness that blocked the warmth of the sun awakened him. Before he opened his eyes he imagined that it must be a cloud passing in front of the sun. He patiently waited for the sun to warm him once again, but the minutes ticked by and the sunlight never returned. He reluctantly opened his eyes to investigate what was going on.

It just so happened that Avery's best friend, Melvin Kolly from next door, had just raised solar panels that blocked almost all of the light from his porch. Like huge billboards, the solar panels stood tall and ominous on the other side of the fence. Melvin's panels siphoned the sunlight from Avery's most favorite place. This was not the first time that Melvin had blocked sunlight from that spot. Over the years he had produced several projects that inadvertently blocked Avery's light. Each time before when Avery had spoken to his friend about how the contraptions blocked his light and warmth, Melvin explained that he had the right to build anything he wanted as long as it was on his side of the fence. Avery tried to explain to his best friend that, though he did in fact build on his own side of the fence, his projects radically affected the sun exposure to his favorite spot on his wrap-around porch, not to mention to the flower garden that required full sun to grow.

Frequently in the past, after Avery had spoken to his friend about how he was blocking the sunlight, Melvin would disappear into his ranch house, not answering the phone

or the door, isolating himself for days on end. However, each time when Melvin emerged from his house he always dismantled the offending building or contraption and the sunlight would once again bathe Avery's porch and garden with its healing warmth.

Today, Avery planned to suggest to Melvin that he move the panels to another location on his ranch, to a place that would be both productive for Melvin and non-intrusive to him. It was, of course, up to Melvin where he moved them, but Avery would suggest that he could install them on the roof of his ranch house where they would have the best opportunity to generate energy for Melvin. However Melvin handled it, Avery's only request was that he move them to a place where they would no longer block the sun from his porch.

Avery knew he had to prepare himself for the chance that Melvin might not choose to move the panels, so before he approached him, he surveyed his own sun porch for possibilities of additional sources of sunlight. Right above the hammock the eaves of the house extended out far enough to cover the entire porch, leaving the sun's warmth to shine from the side. He closed his eyes and imagined two skylights approximately three feet apart, cut right into the eaves. The skylights would let the sun directly in and also allow for very comfortable stargazing from the hammock at night. He smiled and whispered to himself, "There is always a solution." He felt happy just thinking about it. In a split second he decided to make it happen. He called Theo Sage for a consult on the best way to install the skylights, and as usual, Theo offered to help.

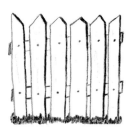

Avery smiled and whispered to himself...
"There is always a solution."

After Avery had gathered all of the necessary materials, Theo joined him and in one day they installed two skylights positioned to bring light and warmth to the porch for the better part of a summer's day. As they relaxed in the porch rocking chairs, admiring their work, Melvin stuck his head over the fence and said, "Sorry about these contraptions. Nice skylights. I could use some of those too." Avery walked over to their adjoining fence and gently offered his idea about moving the solar panels to Melvin's ranch house roof. Tired and worn out, Melvin sighed at the idea of the work it would take to move them. Theo spoke up from the porch and said, "Melvin, I'm here if you need help." Avery nodded and offered his support as well. Melvin said he would let them know and he plodded back to his ranch house and disappeared inside.

Melvin spent weeks holed up in his house while his solar panels still stood like billboards. But Avery enjoyed the full sun on his porch hammock nearly every afternoon. And after dinner most days, he returned to the hammock to gaze at the heavens, marveling at the plethora of twinkling stars and far-away planets. So grateful was he for the new avenues to the heavens that he often quietly thanked Melvin Kolly for making it necessary for him to find this solution. ▪

Sorting Horses

The horses were running wild in the field, kicking up their hooves and screaming. Something was definitely wrong! Avery Soul rushed out of the house with his shotgun in case there were wolves threatening his herd. When he reached the pasture he could not believe his eyes. There were twice as many horses than should have been there, and he could hardly tell his apart from the others. He surveyed the fence that surrounded the pasture as far as he could see. In the distance he saw a portion of a wood and wire gate laying flat on the ground. The section next to it was badly bent and tangled. The lock, which had secured the gate, appeared to have been cut. He could see that it was going to take some extensive work to repair the damage to his fence.

It was clear that the intruding horses were from Barj Inne's Ranch, which connected to his land in only a small corridor. Years before when Avery and Barj had been good friends, they had spent many days talking and laughing and sharing their dreams for the future. In many ways they had been like brothers. So close were they at one time, that Avery had installed a gate between their ranches to allow easy entrance for his friend. For a while everything seemed fine. However, occasionally Avery would find Barj Inne's animals feeding in his pasture with his horses. More than

once Barj's horses had bitten and kicked Avery's horses, making it difficult for them to feed and rest up properly. When Avery approached his friend with the problem, Barj just smiled and said, "Hey, friend, that's the way animals are, the survival of the fittest. Besides, how much have I given you over the years? You owe me a lot. The least you can do is let my animals graze your land."

It was true that Barj had lent him many tools throughout the years and had helped him build his work shed. But Avery had also been there for Barj when he got fired from his job and was down and out. They weren't always tangible things that Avery had given his friend during those tough times, but it was clear that Barj had forgotten the immeasurable care Avery had given freely in the name of friendship. After that, conversation time went by slowly, and the once comfortable friendship became heavy with duties that

Barj believed he had the right to expect of Avery. One day, when Avery finally had had enough, he put a heavy duty lock on the gate that separated his and Barj Inne's ranch.

Today that lock was lying on the ground in pieces, apparently cut by a heavy duty wire cutter, and the gate was twisted and torn. Avery suspected that it was Barj Inne who had cut the lock. The gate had not been opened, instead it looked like the powerful horses had been stampeded and funneled through the corridor to knock the gate down like a tsunami crashing through a town. Avery felt the intentional invasion in his own heart. He considered for a moment that it might all have been an accident, but by the looks of the lock in pieces on the ground, it was clear it was deliberate. No matter what the cause, the result was disastrous. Avery knew that he needed to send Barj's horses home and fortify his fence to prevent any further intrusion. But when he started to round them up, he found it hard

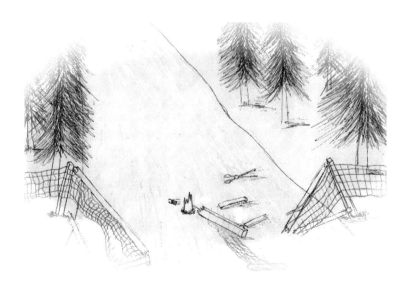

Avery realized that it was up to him to sort out what was his and what wasn't.

to distinguish Barj's horses from his own. He attempted to enlist Barj's help in identifying his herd, but unfortunately he was conveniently unavailable. Avery realized it was up to him to sort out what was his and what wasn't. He had to do the work himself. All morning long he watched the horses as they moved around the pasture. He still had a difficult time distinguishing his horses from the intruders. They looked so similar. He began to sort his out by calling out the nicknames he had for each of his horses. Many came to him immediately when they heard his familiar call. Others did not respond. He then tried his special whistle that sounded a lot like a high pitched, shrill voice singing "yoooou-whooooo!" A few more of his herd trotted over. As each horse came to him, he led them into a part of the pasture that he had sectioned off with a makeshift rope fence. By mid-afternoon most of his horses had been safely gathered, but there were a few more horses he needed to find. He decided the best way to identify them was to watch them closely for their unique ways of moving. Another hour passed before Avery was certain he had his whole herd separated from Barj Inne's horses.

The next job was rounding up Barj's herd and driving them back where they belonged. That proved easier than he had anticipated. With his trusty herding dogs and his cutting horse, the intruders were escorted back to their land in less than half an hour.

The last job was securing the fence between the ranches to prevent any further intrusions. Avery surveyed the damage to the fence once again and made a plan. He discovered that the original wood posts that anchored the fence, were

too shallow and too weak. Along the fence line he added more posts and replaced the wood with high grade stainless steel. He dug the post holes two feet deeper than before and filled them with quick drying cement. He reattached the fence wire and for good measure, added a second layer of wire to fortify it.

When he was finished, the fence, no longer a gate, was so strong that it would take a bulldozer to push it down. He was relieved and tired after the long day, but he felt a strong sense of safety and confidence. He took down the temporary rope fence to allow his herd to once again graze freely in the field. There was something so comforting about having his horses safe and sound in their own pasture. He felt relieved and at home, as he leaned on a rock in the middle of the field, surrounded by his horses. He sighed contentedly as he watched the sun sink slowly from the sky. ◼

The Magnificent Filtering Wall

Avery Soul met up with a long-time neighbor, Trixie Rager, as he was tending his exotic flower garden along their ranch border. Suddenly, without warning or provocation, she began to yell at him in a tirade of such hurtful words that he was shell shocked. Stunned by her outburst he stood perfectly still, paralyzed with emotion. Then, out of the corner of his eye, he noticed that the fence that joined their two ranches had given way to a flood from Trixie Rager's slimy, toxic pond. For some unknown reason she had decided to remove the stones, dirt and wood that for years had acted like a dam for the pond that was fed by an old creek that ran through her property. The stagnant pond sat several feet above Avery's border and unfortunately, the foul water was gushing over what was left of that wall, tearing down the fence and flooding Avery's flower garden with the noxious water. Mosquitoes, larvae and bacteria of all kinds forged a muddy path onto his ranch, wreaking havoc on what he had spent years nurturing. Bewildered by Trixie Rager's actions, Avery stood very still, hardly breathing, as he considered his options.

He imagined himself marching up to where the fence once was and yelling at his neighbor, "How dare you do this! You had no right to flood my land. You are ruining my tender seedlings and delicate flowers." Then he thought to

himself, "What would that accomplish? Trixie is well known for her advanced abilities to retaliate and make it look like it wasn't her fault. Angry words from me would mean that she got to me and reduced me to upset. She seems to delight in that sort of game and I do not want to play."

He considered another approach. He could talk to some of the other neighbors and try to rally support against her. "No," he whispered to himself. When he thought it through, that didn't seem right either. It would be like creating a mob mentality, and though she had many, shall we say, disgruntled acquaintances, he felt that this problem was just between the two of them. He really didn't want to complicate it any further by bringing someone else into it. However, he reserved the right to seek help from others if nothing else worked to solve the problem. For a moment he even considered calling the police or getting a lawyer to sue. But he wanted to try another remedy first.

Avery took a deep breath and forced himself to look at the situation from a different perspective. As he wondered how he could make good from it, he stood back and imagined building a new, stronger, higher wall with an integrated filtering system to sort the clean water from the scum. The fence he envisioned would allow a trickle of water through to feed his delicate garden, but it would keep out slime. Then he mulled over what he wanted to say to her about his new idea. Maybe . . . "Your pond water is flooding and killing my garden. Though I'm going to build a new filtering wall to keep the slime and bacteria from your pond out of my garden, I would be happy to receive pure, clean water for my flowers. My built-in filtering system will allow for this." He noted that she would need to deal with the slime on her side, and that was her business.

Yes, this is what he would do. He approached Trixie Rager, who had an odd, yet snide grin on her face that said, "Game on!" Avery told her of his plan and she was so surprised that her nasty grin fell into a full open, speechless mouth. As he finished and walked away to begin work on the wall, she whispered angrily to herself, " Who is this guy? Who does he think he is?" She stomped back to her house in a huff to regroup and redouble her efforts.

Before Avery hiked back to his ranch house to begin sketching the design for the filtering wall, he devised a temporary redirect to shoot the water off to the side around and way from the flowers. Once that was accomplished he set about sketching the design out on paper, with a plan that would use all natural materials. He was sure that he had most of the supplies he needed already on his land. It took

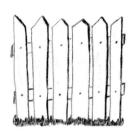

Avery took a deep breath and forced
himself to look at the situation from
a different perspective,
believing he could make good of it.

many hours of back-breaking work and buckets of sweat to gather the materials he needed from the vast areas of his ranch. When they were all assembled into organized piles near the building site, Avery began to build what turned out to be a magnificent filtering wall. It consisted of several beautiful, multi-hued boulders, and shiny, colorful rocks that had been smoothed and painted by the soil and water of his own land. Like the pieces of a puzzle he arranged the materials into a wall held together by mortar made of sand from a dry brook on his ranch. In the middle of the wall he placed layers of smaller rocks and pebbles, each with their own particular crevice, leaving only tiny holes to filter the pond flow into pure and useful water.

When he was finished, the wall stood nearly fifteen feet high and twenty feet long, spanning the entire length of Trixie Rager's ranch connection to his property. It was stunningly beautiful and ingenious. Even Trixie commented that she

Avery began to build what turned out
to be a magnificent filtering wall, that
kept the sludge and slime out and
let clean, pure water through.

liked it very much. Avery was pleased with the outcome of his hard work, and his flowers eventually flourished.

A day or two after he finished the filtering wall, he was sitting in his favorite chair on the back porch, thinking to himself. He said out loud to no one there, "Trixie Rager may try to flood my land again, but I know now that I can always change my side of the fence to protect and nurture my ranch." He didn't mind the hard work involved in building the wall. In fact, he was a bit grateful for the opportunity the event presented that allowed him to use his creativity to solve the problem. Because of his ingenuity at facing and solving this challenge, he knew he could handle whatever came next.

Angel Goodheart

A very Soul found himself chronically wide awake in the wee hours of the morning, and he began to worry that he would never sleep through the night again. Each night for the past two weeks when he lay down ready to sleep, his friend and neighbor Angel Goodheart floated into his mind. It all started a few weeks before when Avery was out walking to get some fresh air and had taken an old familiar path on his ranch that he hadn't followed in a while. The path he took led to a place where his and Angel Goodheart's ranches met at a broken split rail fence. It was innocent enough when he stopped to talk with Angel that day. She was undertaking the huge project of redesigning and improving her ranch house.

At first Avery just leaned comfortably against the old wooden fence that separated their ranches, and listened as she described the plans for her project in detail. Through the years Avery had come to know Angel's style for attacking new ideas. She was the sort of person who jumped in with both feet. Though most often her ideas had proven to be ingenious and quite successful, sometimes she found herself desperately trapped in a compromising position. Avery loved and admired his friend for her willingness to dare greatly, and he was always supportive and amazed at her efforts.

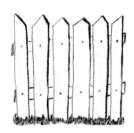

Before he knew it, Avery had easily hopped over the old, crumbling fence and was walking around Angel's ranch as if he was the construction foreman.

That day as Avery listened intently to Angel describe how she would change the structure and decor of her ranch house, he was picturing easier and more efficient ways she could use to rebuild. Before he knew it, Avery had easily hopped over the old, crumbling fence and was walking around Angel's ranch as if he was the construction foreman. He proceeded to give Angel many new ideas and show her a myriad of different ways to do things she had already started. Walking around and feeling his creativity and experience flowing, he reveled in being a major player in Angel's ranch house improvements. On the surface Angel seemed grateful for Avery's input, but inside she suddenly felt small and inept.

Avery lay awake every night thinking of new and better ways to reconstruct Angel's ranch house. He felt exhilarated at first, but this particular night he began to notice how much time he was dedicating to thinking about her project. After

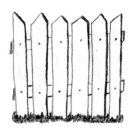

On the surface, Angel Goodheart
seemed grateful for Avery's input,
but inside she suddenly
felt

small

and

inept.

two weeks of no sleep he began to feel a sense of urgency for Angel to finish her project so things could get back to normal. Every night after Avery had spent the majority of his day on Angel's project, he was so exhausted he let his own house fall into disarray. Clutter, chores, and fix it jobs were left undone until he began to feel overwhelmed in his own house. As he lay awake this night thinking the whole thing through, he began to feel the heat of embarrassment creep over him as he realized that he had bullied his way into Angel's project, to the detriment of his own house and life. He decided to gather himself back up and focus on putting his own house in order. Even with his resolve to stay on his side, he was so drawn to the gap in the fence between their ranches because a part of him was still passionate about the work she was doing. Avery's goal had been to make sure that Angel's ranch house was exquisite and useful. But now he had a new goal . . . to trust that she could do that for herself. He realized that though his intentions seemed honorable, his involvement in her project had consumed him and deflated Angel. He needed to stop himself from going any further lest he ruin their friendship.

He knew he needed to apologize to Angel for intruding on her project. So he met up with her at the fence and told her how very sorry he was for jumping over their broken fence, and promised to rebuild it higher and stronger. Since Avery deeply valued his friendship with Angel, he still wanted to meet her at the fence occasionally. So he decided to build a comfortable bench on his side of the fence where he could still sit and listen to Angel as she described her renovation without interference from him. He knew that Angel would

want to hear about changes on his ranch house too, as he put it back in order.

Once Avery drew up the plans for the fence, he gathered the materials and started to build. He brought redwood rails for the fence and oak to build his bench. Avery worked from morning until dusk, and by the day's end he was sitting cozily on the new bench on his side of the freshly built fence. Angel Goodheart joined him and leaned contentedly on her side of the fence. The two friends talked late into the night sharing ideas and gazing at the same starry sky from their own vantage points. That night when Avery's head hit his pillow, he fell soundly to sleep dreaming of his own ranch house and the plans he had to improve it. ▧

The Shrinking Fence

The old cobblestone fence was about hip height to Avery and sprinkled with weeds and ivy. It divided the land into three sections, one belonging to Avery Soul, one to Skip Owt and the third to Sissy Neaner. Long ago when Avery was a child, he had come to the fence with openness and innocence, ready to offer his true friendship. But every time he met there with Skip and Sissy, he felt himself shrink smaller and smaller until his head barely met the top of the fence. Not able to see him anymore, Skip and Sissy would leave together to play and tell secrets.

As he got older, Avery noticed that he still shrank as he neared this particular fence, and he always turned away from it feeling dejected and left out. But as time went by he also noticed that as he walked away from the fence towards his ranch house he grew and grew until he was his normal, comfortable height.

For many years he shied away from the cobblestone fence. But one night he dreamt about those two neighbors and he woke up feeling curious about seeing the fence again. In his dream, like every time before when he approached the fence, he began to shrink. Still dreaming, he experimented with how close he could get to the cobblestone fence

before he began to shrink. At first, he moved too close and shrank to three quarters size. He backed off to recover to his normal self, and then he tried it again but not as close. The same thing happened, but he shrank only a little and recovered faster. The next time Avery stepped forward, he closed his eyes and told himself, "Tell me when to stop." And so as often happened when he trusted himself, he found he already knew the answer. He took small steps, one at a time, listening for his inner voice. After three small steps he told himself, "Here, stop here!" He opened his eyes to find himself approximately 50 feet from the cobblestone fence where Skip and Sissy were whispering and chatting with each other as usual. He felt safe and content from the new distance.

When he woke from his dream he decided to go to the cobblestone fence and actually measure 50 feet back and

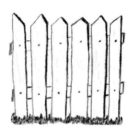

As often happened
when he trusted himself...
he found he already knew the answer.

build another fence. The trouble was that as always happened before, when he approached the fence to start counting the 50 feet backward, he shrank as he had in his dream. It took him nearly a full day of shrinking and recovering to do the measuring, but he managed to finish it. After a good night's rest he got up the next morning to work on building another fence at the new location. This one was cobblestone too, but taller and more beautiful than the other one. It created a space of 50 feet by 100 feet between the two fences, a buffer of sorts.

A funny thing happened once Avery finished the fence . . . Sissy and Skip finally saw him and waved to him. He waved back, happy to finally be seen, but he never got closer than his side of the new fence. ■

A funny thing happened once
Avery had finished his fence...

Sissy and Skip finally saw him.

■ ■ ■
Close the Gate

A mountain of catalogs and shiny brochures were strewn all over the dining room table, chairs and floor like a breakaway dam. Avery was in the market for a new tractor with all the bells and whistles and he was like a bloodhound on the hunt. He had dreamed of his perfect tractor for years as he sat atop his trusty, but overworked shiny red rig. He treated his tractor more like a prized racecar, washing and polishing it every week, tuning it up so it would always run at its top potential.

But even at its best, it could only do so much. He needed something to better meet the needs of his ever-changing ranch, one that could haul heavy loads of materials from one end of his ranch to the other as he put things in order. And since he spent so much time on his tractor at the mercy of the elements, he promised himself that his next one would have a tempered-glass enclosed, air-conditioned cab with an excellent sound system, and a mini-refrigerator. After all, he spent more time on his tractor than he did in his truck, and he figured he might as well be comfortable. He had spent hours and days leafing through the catalogs and had taken a few trips to the tractor lot where he saw firsthand what the new tractors could do. He finally decided on one that met all of his needs and desires for comfort, power and durability, but mostly versatility.

As he placed his order and secured payment for his new tractor, his stomach did a flip for joy. The feeling reminded him of his fifth birthday when he received his most prized possessions, a bright yellow Tonka tractor and dump truck to match. He got lost in the memory of playing in the dirt pile on the side yard of his childhood home. He could almost smell the wholesomeness of the soft, dark dirt that he had scooped and dumped as he moved things around in his tiny corner of the world. Drifting out of the daze of the long-ago memory, he found himself in front of the life-sized version of his Tonka, only it was deep green with thin yellow and red pinstriped lines and letters. He climbed up into the cab that had all the features he had wanted, including a seat heater for the cold days, and it felt like home. He made his decision on the spot, finalizing it with payment in full to place the order.

A few days later, after he had given his old tractor a good tune up and a fresh buffing of wax, he parked it in the front yard of his ranch house and put a large "For Sale" sign on it with all of his contact information. Rather than advertise in the newspaper or on the Internet, he had decided to park it just inside the white picket fence that separated his ranch from the common street. Cars often drove down his street and he hoped that some passerby might see it and be interested in buying it.

Just as he had thought, and in record time, a fellow from down the street showed up to check out the tractor. Myne Memine unlatched and walked through the gate to get a closer look. Avery happened to be passing through the front room of his ranch house and saw Myne through his front window, climbing up onto the tractor seat. He winced for a moment at the thought of his neighbor letting himself in the gate, and went out to meet him. He motioned to Myne to climb down so they could chat. Avery explained to Myne Memine that he was going into town for a few hours and that upon his return he would be happy to let him take a test drive. With that the two ranchers went their separate

ways. As Avery pulled out of his driveway, he closed but did not lock the gate behind him. He was sure his place would be safe.

An hour or so after Avery had left for town, Myne returned and opened the front gate to get to the tractor. He justified that the tractor was going to be his, since he intended to buy it, so he hopped right up onto the seat, started up the engine, and drove it right down the street to his own ranch. Since he had it, he thought he might as well try it out on his field. So for nearly an hour, Myne Memine used Avery's tractor without a care in the world. When Avery returned to see his gate open, tractor gone, and muddy tire marks leading all the way to Myne Memine's ranch, he was floored. He followed the trail to the Memine ranch, and he couldn't believe his eyes. Myne Memine had finished plowing his small field and Avery's tractor was muddy and nearly out of gas. Not to mention that it was no longer safely parked in his front yard.

Avery tromped out to the field to have a stern word with Myne, who almost ran him over. When Myne saw Avery, he stopped, but kept the engine idling as if nothing at all was wrong. Avery motioned to him to cut the engine, which he did, however he remained in the tractor seat high above Avery. Shielding his eyes from the high noon sun, he told Myne in no uncertain terms that he had explicitly instructed him that he could test drive the tractor when he returned from town. He added, "The fact that you took the tractor without asking cancels any possibility of me selling it to you now." Myne argued that since he had fully intended to buy the tractor, he saw there was no harm done. Avery

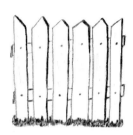

"The fact that you don't see the harm in
what you have done, only makes it worse.
Get down off of the tractor
and hand over the keys.

We are finished here."

responded by saying, "The fact that you don't see the harm in what you have done makes it worse. Get down off of the tractor and hand over the keys. We are finished here." Then he added, "When you respect me and my property, I'll consider the same for you."

Myne Memine did not really understand what the big deal was. He thought to himself, "So what if I drove the tractor without permission, its not like I stole it. I had intended on buying it, and it was sitting right out there, ripe for the picking." As Avery drove his tractor off the field and onto the road heading back to his ranch, Myne yelled to him that he was being unfair and oversensitive. Myne then mumbled under his breath that he would find a better tractor anyhow, though he wasn't sure where.

As Avery Soul drove the tractor through the gate and parked it back where it had been, he thought to himself that he was partially to blame for neglecting to secure the gate when he left. Later that day the tractor was cleaned up and once again on display. And the next day he installed

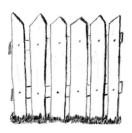

As Avery Soul drove the tractor
through the gate and parked it back
where it had been, he thought to himself
that he was partially responsible for
neglecting to secure his gate.

an automatic gate opener that kept the gate secured with a push of a button. As he was testing it, Avery noticed another neighbor standing across the street from his front yard. Tru Onnor was slowly walking back and forth to get different perspectives of the tractor from a distance. Tru had always admired Avery's tractor and he knew that he took pristine care of it. In fact, he had hoped to own a tractor like this one some day. He imagined himself sitting up on the seat, driving the tractor around his ranch, tuning it up on a regular basis, and washing and polishing it to keep it safe from the elements. He was so deep in thought that he didn't notice that Avery had walked up to the front fence to speak to him. Avery said, "You looking at the tractor?" Startled, Tru responded, "It's a beauty! I have always admired it." Avery pulled the keys from his pocket and tossed them over to Tru who had joined him at the fence. "Care to take it for a spin?"

Tru's eyes lit up. "Yes! If you don't mind." Not only did Avery not mind, he totally appreciated Tru Onnor's respect and enthusiasm. Tru drove the tractor out the gate and onto the street and took it for a short test drive. Within a few minutes, Tru came back and told Avery he wanted to buy it. They settled on a fair price and Avery bid goodbye to his old tractor. He smiled as Tru Onnor drove it away, knowing that his trusty tractor was in excellent hands.

The next morning the rumble of a big truck idling in front of his house awakened Avery. Before he could finish dressing, he heard the deep, loud sound of the semi truck's horn and it made him jump for joy. His new tractor had arrived! It took a little while to unload it from the trailer along with all of its specially ordered attachments. It was like his fifth birthday all over again. He was pleased with his new tractor, and even more pleased that his trusty old tractor would be well taken care of and put to good use. ▥

Four Corners

There was a place on Avery Soul's ranch that met up with three other ranches belonging to his neighbors: Alvin Schemer, Timmy Trueblue, and Sam Noble. Every once in a while the four neighbors would find themselves coincidentally convened there. They were an interesting bunch. Avery, a rancher who cared well for his loved ones and his land; Sam, an astronaut and adventurer; Timmy a former pro hockey player who became a sports psychologist; and Alvin, a slick used car salesman turned unethical and dishonest lawyer. Avery always enjoyed the company of Sam Noble as he was friendly and kept the conversation interesting. He often found that his time with Timmy went

Alvin Schemer was big on mind
games and strategic tactics that put
him in control, particularly the
"divide and conquer" maneuver.
Avery was always on guard around him.

by way too fast because Timmy was so refreshingly genuine, engaging and fun to be with. He was caring and passionate about life and Avery always felt energized and inspired after spending time with him. Alvin Schemer was a different story. He was outgoing and liked listening to the sound of his own voice. He was big on mind games and strategic tactics that put him in control, particularly the 'divide and conquer' maneuver. Avery was always on guard with him.

When Avery, Sam and Timmy met together at the Four Corners fence their time was uplifting and comfortable. They told funny stories and occasionally shared the quiet of the day. They did not always have to talk, sometimes they just enjoyed one another's company. When Alvin Schemer joined them, however everything changed. He had gates installed years before that opened onto the other three ranches. Invariably he would come to the Four Corners and invite one or two of the three neighbors to join him on his land, always leaving someone out. Or he would open his gate and

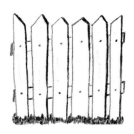

Avery learned long ago that his
fence, where it adjoined to
Alvin's land, needed to be secure.

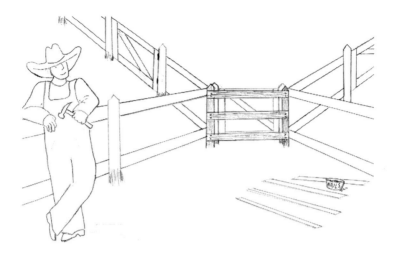

enter the property of one of the others, luring them away. Alvin Schemer was a convincing fellow. He could sell any-thing, product or idea, to anyone, and have them convinced, at least for a while, that he was doing them a great favor.

Avery had learned long ago that his fence, where it adjoined Alvin's land, needed to be secure. He built it dou-bly thick making it impossible for Alvin's gate to open onto his ranch uninvited. He saw how the others were dragged into conversations and projects in which they were not interested, because they didn't know how to avoid being steamrolled by Alvin. He could protect himself from Alvin's manipulations, but he could do nothing to make it safe for Sam and Timmy. Though Avery was always there for his two friends, he knew they would need to learn to fortify their own fences. ■

Giving on Empty

Avery Soul had a small orchard with some of the healthiest and abundant orange trees in his town. As an offering of holy thanksgiving for such a lovely treasure of a grove, he would give his sweetest and juiciest oranges as gifts to his friends and neighbors. He kept a small amount for himself and his family and he took the remainder of his delicious crop to the Farmers Market, where people often clamored to buy them as he arrived.

Avery's orange crops had a stellar reputation. For years they provided exceptional nourishment to the people of his town. Year after year he packed up lovely baskets full of the oranges to give to his people. At first, they had thanked him graciously, so touched by his generosity. But as the years went by they came to expect the oranges, and what had started as an act of loving kindness, soon became an obligation. Not only that, but each year more and more friends demanded to be on the "giveaway" list. Soon Avery's load of oranges for the Farmers Market dwindled to only a few bushel baskets and then, finally, he had to put his own share in to sell.

When it was again time to harvest oranges, what had once been a joy was now a dread. The whole thing had become tiresome and disappointing, out of hand, really.

In the last few years as he surveyed his orange crop before harvest, he noticed the trees were beginning to dry up and whither a bit. There had been too little rain and not enough good sunlight for a few years straight, and it was beginning to take its toll. Each year's harvest was noticeably smaller than the year before. So as he dutifully packed what had become a ridiculous number of gift baskets of oranges, he put fewer oranges in each basket. When he went out to distribute the gift baskets to his friends and neighbors, he was too often met with disappointment and even insult. "We count on these oranges to get us through cold and flu season. How can you give us so little?"

Avery was completely dumbfounded by some of the blatant statements his people made. "This is not enough!" "You are being selfish!" "Is that all there is?" And so on.

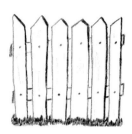

What started as an act of loving kindness,
soon became a burdensome obligation.

"We count on the oranges to get us
through the cold and flu season.
How dare you give us so little!"

By the time he returned home from his deliveries he was exhausted and defeated. As the days moved by he became angry and despondent. And as the years passed his orange grove grew sicker and sicker, yielding fewer and smaller fruits. Avery was so saddened by the state of his grove and he did everything he could to save it. He consulted experts to no avail, until it became clear that the grove had spent itself.

One foggy, cold night Avery wrapped himself in his favorite blue flannel blanket and went for a walk in his orange grove. He lit a torch that both warmed him and shined on his path. As he wandered among the trees he could see that they were twisted and mangled as if they were trying to squeeze out the very best of what they had left, to give the last of their fruit.

Avery spoke to the trees and thanked them for all they had given through the years. He shared with them his sadness and confusion about people's expectations. Avery was quiet for a long time, soothed by the trees that seemed to understand him. As the torch burned out, Avery leaned against one of the trees, and pulling his blanket close around him, fell into a deep sleep during which he had a dream . . .

He was in the kitchen squeezing homemade orange juice. The smell of the freshly squeezed oranges permeated the ranch house and wafted on the lovely warm breeze that blew through the window. He was alone and deep in thought. Suddenly, he was startled by a knock on the door. He quickly washed his hands and dried them on a soft kitchen towel. He was still holding the towel when he answered the door. It was his friend, Mo. They had grown up together and knew each other as well as they knew themselves.

Mo was both a talented gardener and a gourmet cook and baker. He had just harvested zucchini from his garden and had made his famous zucchini bread to share with Avery. Avery was delighted and invited him in for a morning snack. Avery poured his freshly squeezed orange juice and Mo sliced the just out of the oven, warm, sweet zucchini bread. They sat on the sun porch for a visit while they enjoyed the tasty morsels of their healthy and delicious snack.

The two friends were quiet for a while and then Mo asked, "What have you been doing lately?" Avery paused, sighing deeply, and said, "It seems like I have been picking oranges from sun up to sun down." He paused and then added, "And I've been thinking." Mo nodded "Yeah, I thought so." He smiled at Avery for they had been friends long enough that he could tell when Avery was lost in the recesses of his own mind. He didn't ask what he was thinking about. Instead he told him a story.

"My friend," he said, "I have spent a long time in my garden through the years. And my biggest challenge has been the little critters that help themselves to my growing vegetables. Now, these rabbits and gophers and deer are all God's creatures for sure, but they were ruining my crops and leaving very little for my family and me. I knew I had to do something about the inequity. So, one day I sat in the middle of my garden all day and through the night, thinking about what I could do to feed both my family and the critters. The answer came as I watched the rabbits munching

on my beautiful romaine lettuce. The truth is I got mad and shoed them all away. I didn't want them in or near my garden at all. They were taking what was not intended for them. I decided to build an impenetrable fence that had both beauty and purpose. The next morning I devised a plan and gathered the necessary materials. I drew a design, measured and began to build it. It was a picket fence with clear wire fencing filling the space between the slats. I dug a trench a few feet deep and secured the fence in cement all the way around it, then covered the cement with dirt. I worked for several days to finish it. When it was completed, I was pleased with the results of my hard work. No critters could get in. And no birds could pick at them from above as I had draped and secured a fine mesh across the top of the fence slats, far above the tallest corn stalks. Now as I pick my vegetables I can decide what, if any, I will share with my animal friends."

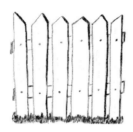

"With each attempt they showed another
flaw in my design. And with each flaw
I designed a solution until the
whole garden fence was fool proof.
In a way, they were my greatest teachers."

Avery sat quietly for a while, then he inquired. "Did the animals ever seem angry?" "Funny you should ask that. They came in large numbers for the days and nights that followed and forcefully tried every way they could to get back into the garden. With each attempt they showed me another flaw in my design. And with each flaw I designed a solution until the whole garden fence was foolproof. In a way, they were my greatest teachers."

Avery was deep in thought. When he finally looked up again to see Mo, he found himself alone laying in the middle of his orange grove wrapped snugly in his blue flannel blanket. He lay there for a long time pondering his dream. As the sun came up Avery heard the birds singing cheerfully in the tree above him. It was cold, he thought, for birds to be out at all. But they were there as if to cheer him on.

He made a decision then and there. He decided his orange grove needed a break. The trees needed special treatment to bring them back to health. Trusting his own ingenuity

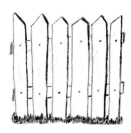

Avery simply said, "No."

and talents for combining nutrients and soil enhancements, he hoped to support and heal the trees. As he started the healing process he watered the trees more often, walked among them and spoke encouraging words to them. He knew these trees as if they were people and they seemed to know and trust him. After a while they came back to life.

A few years went by in which Avery gave no oranges away. The trees were still healing. The first year friends and neighbors were angry and disappointed. Avery listened, but firmly stated, "Not this year. The trees need time to heal and renew." They looked at him like he was crazy and argued further. Avery then simply said, "NO!"

The second year his friends noticed there still were no gift baskets of oranges, but they didn't say much about it. By the third year the orange trees began to blossom and yield fruit again. However, he still said "No," when asked about the gift baskets. He had learned so much from the whole experience, not the least of which was that giving must always come from a pure heart, without imposed expectations. Anything other than that is not giving, its draining. ▨

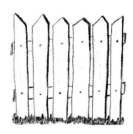

True giving always comes from a
pure heart, without imposed expectations.
Anything else is not so much giving,

as

it

is

draining.

■ ■ ■

Runaway Ivy

I t had rained for several days and Avery Soul was unable
to tend to his ranch in his usual manner. "Rain is good for
all growing things," he had said to himself as he sat down
to read his favorite book. He read this same book about
building fences and walls, patios and gazebos, and gardening every chance he got. He loved to look at the pictures
and diagrams that gave him new ideas for his ranch. And
on this rainy day, his house was in order and the weather
provided the perfect excuse. He was reading the chapter
about climbing vines and ground covers as he had been
battling a particularly invasive ivy that came from the yard
of Al Consuming. He'd tried many ways to contain it or get
rid of it. The problem was that it grew so fast he couldn't
keep up with it and it invaded most anything that got in its
way. And as pretty as it was, it was not what he wanted in
his varietal fruit tree orchard that was located on his side
of the fence just below the neighbor's ranch.

A few years before, Al Consuming had spoken to Avery
on several occasions about a patch of bare land in their
yard that didn't seem to be able to sustain any growth.
Avery suggested that he look into a hearty ground cover.
Apparently they had taken his advice and planted a lovely,
small, variegated ivy. It did the trick and covered the bare

spot quickly and completely, but then it began to sneak over the small fence between their ranches.

As time went by the ivy became a problem for Al and his wife, Alice, as well as for Avery who had to cut it back nearly every single day just to keep it from taking over his land. Luckily when the Consumings decided to put in a pool earlier that year, the law stated that they were required to raise the fence to over six feet. And when they did so, they also pulled the ivy off the fence and cut it back. Avery was so pleased since it meant that he didn't have to keep cutting it back on his side of the fence.

Unfortunately, a few weeks after the fence was completed the ivy returned in full force and having reached the top of the new fence, it spilled over and spread like a wildfire into his small orchard. The fruit trees closest to the fence were one by one squeezed out. The ivy seemed to grow by leaps and bounds during the night, twisting and turning on the ground, up the small trunks and down the tender branches where the fruit struggled to grow. Very quickly the ivy took over, leaving no room for the fruit. Avery had to do something and fast, for not only had the ivy invaded the fruit trees, it also was taking over his kids' play yard structure. The small orchard and play yard shared a sloping berm that included a large flat pad at the top on Avery's side of the fence. The play yard was a two-story fort with a long slide that traveled down to the bottom of the slope. It was so fun to ride that Avery often rewarded himself with a fast trip down the slide at the end of a hard day's work. Now, though, as he surveyed the ivy invasion, he noticed that it was starting to damage the fort and slide.

He had spoken to Al Consuming about the ivy, but he said there was nothing they could do about it since their yard was taken over by the large pool construction equipment. He also confessed to Avery that the process was taking longer than they had anticipated. The pool builders had unearthed many interesting items while digging the hole for the pool. Some of the items belonged to Al and Alice, most likely buried long ago by their dog. Some of the items belonged to the former owner and the original builders who had long since gone. Entranced by the finds from their yard, Al and Alice saved all of the items to examine for posterity and worth. Meanwhile the ivy they had planted was going untended and pouring through Avery's fence like a gushing waterfall. With the deep hole in the ground and the large construction equipment around, the Consumings could not reach the ivy to cut it back. It was clear that it was up to Avery to get it under control to protect his ranch and orchard.

And so, on this rainy day he took the time to arm himself with knowledge and practical information about the nature of ivy. It was interesting but fairly disheartening, for he found that short of continually cutting it back or using dangerous chemicals to kill it altogether, there was little else he could do. Using chemicals did not settle well with Avery because they harmed the earth for generations. Cutting it back had become nearly a full time job, and since he had many other responsibilities on his ranch to attend to, he could not continue to give all of his time to the ivy situation. He knew there had to be a better way. So he called and consulted with an expert who told him that this ivy would not grow across a body of water and would not flourish in sand. It was worth a try, so Avery took the rest of the day to create a workable plan to contain the problem.

The next day, when the sun was shining and drying up the land, he set out to put his plan into action. He used his tractor to transport the sand, river rocks and stones from the old dried-up stream that once flowed through his land. Over a week's time he worked all day and into the evening. He started by moving ten of the fifty trees from the top of the slope down to the base where he kept them in water until the area was ready for planting. Then he dug an eight-foot wide, three-foot deep streambed, ten feet in from the fence all along the connection between the two ranches. He created a small sandy beach on both sides of the stream with the sand and rocks he had hauled. He also moved several boulders and planted hearty, wild, tall grasses in select areas along the creekside to add beauty and natural seating areas. He had designed the water flow of the stream to originate at the natural pond that was at the bottom of the slope. He used a heavy duty pump to send the bubbling water up through pipes he had buried in the hillside, and into the river rock lined stream bed at the top of the slope. He wound the stream around the back of the play yard and down the slope again where it fed back into the pond. Once the water was moving he studied the flow to gauge where to set the pump level. To his surprise and joy, it worked very well.

On the last day he cut back the remaining ivy that hadn't been pulled out while digging the streambed. He poured a mound of sand from the fence to the stream, and spread it out to complete his little beach. He did the same thing on the other side of the stream. Then he took the ten trees that had been soaking in vitamin rich water and planted them in the lower part of the orchard where he could give them special attention until they could bear fruit again. The two-story play fort did not have to be moved, but Avery had to painstakingly cut and pull every bit of ivy from the wood and surrounding area. The stream that wound around the back and side of the fort added another adventurous side-show to the fun zone. He built a new slide that ran down the slope from the second story of the fort and emptied into the lower pond for a refreshing dip. The original slide veered off to the side to land on dry ground.

After his job was done, he settled into his favorite Adirondack chair and took in the fruits of his labor. Not only had he taken care of the invasive ivy issue, but the result was beautiful and useful in ways that exceeded his expectations. As he sat and relaxed, he realized he wasn't quite finished with his job. As he closed his eyes to imagine, he visualized two structures: one spanning the lower pond, and the other high up on the hill over the stream. For the lower structure he envisioned a covered bridge in which he planned to build comfortable benches for shaded respite amid the filtered sunlight. He pictured the upper structure as a gazebo that would overlook his whole ranch. That night he sketched out the plans, drawing from other structures he had made before, and from pictures he had marked in his favorite books.

A few weeks later he finished the covered bridge complete with decorative lattice ends. He planted manageable climbing vines on either side of the bridge and weaved the branches into the lattice. He imagined that by the next Spring the bridge would be covered with the striking blue and purple of the morning glory vines. He looked forward to sitting in the comfort and safety of the flower-covered cocoon in those times when he most needed quiet.

He waited a while to start the next building project because he needed to rest. When Avery was rejuvenated and welling up with excitement for the gazebo project he knew it was time to start. The materials, which had been assembled and waiting since he finished the covered bridge, were ready to be utilized. He hauled them up to the hilltop site by way of a small easement road he had made while constructing the stream. He built the ten-foot round gazebo with great care and with triple reinforcement since it was often quite windy up high on the hill. He placed support beams every two and a half feet and adorned them with decorative ironwork for extra support. He installed a comfy

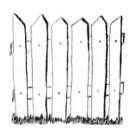

As he surveyed his land from this bird's
eyes view, Avery saw a continuum
of different fences and walls, each
representing a different relationship.

swing bench suspended from a beautiful domed top and sloped roof. When it was completed, the gazebo took in the panoramic view of Avery's entire ranch. As he sat for the first time in the swing to take in the sights, he noticed something from this new perspective that he had never really seen before. "This is almost funny and quite a piece of art," he thought to himself. As he surveyed his land from this birds-eye view he saw a continuum of different fences and walls as far as his eyes could see.

The fence that was most prominent was the fifteen-foot tall double reinforced plank fence he built the day it rained dung from Bubba Bueser's yard. Avery quickly got lost in the memory of the battle he and Theo Sage had fought and won together. For days and weeks after the fence was completed

he could still hear the "Chuff . . . plop" of Bub's shovel as he continually tried to hurl his dung over the fence. The fence was strong and the message was clear, "Don't dump your dung on me!"

Further down the perimeter of his ranch was the Magnificent Filtering Wall, both beautiful and useful. It was perhaps the most difficult to build since he had to contend with the slimy water that flowed from Trixie Rager's stagnant pond. He remembered how he had taken the time to fit every stone and pebble into place to insure that the trickles of water allowed to come through would be pure and clean for his delicate flower garden. He smiled as he realized that he and Trixie had become friends of a sort through the years, as she had grown to respect the clear message he had built, and he had come to see the best in her. The wall was a masterpiece and a reminder of the hard-working nature of their connection.

Avery gazed over at the rooftop of the ranch house that he had rebuilt under the guidance of Theo Sage. He remembered how the torrents of rain had poured through the holes in his broken roof. The whole fiasco had turned into a blessing as Avery had not only learned to fix his roof and repair and remodel the interior of the house, but he had begun a friendship that he now treasured. He sighed with gratitude for all he had learned from Theo about repairing and building fences and structures, both physical ones and those of the heart and mind.

He scanned the horizon and his eyes fixed on the strong steel reinforced fence built at the property line of Barj Inne's ranch. He thought of how fences both connect and protect

He walked back to his ranch house to rest
up for whatever tomorrow would bring,
confident that he could meet it with the
same resourcefulness and strength
from all that he had learned.

us all. "Sometimes," he whispered, "I need to build fences to protect myself and my ranch from my neighbors. And sometimes I need to build them to protect others from my intrusions. Fences strengthen good friendships and set harmful ones straight." As he looked around one last time he smiled and sighed realizing that, though building good boundaries in relationships can be hard work, it is well worth it in the long run. With that, he launched himself off of the swing, climbed out of the gazebo and jogged over to the play yard, where he jumped on the slide and rode quickly to the bottom of the hill. He landed on dry land with his feet firmly planted beneath him. He walked back to the ranch house to rest up for what tomorrow would bring, confident that he could meet it with resourcefulness and strength from all that he had learned. ■

CPSIA information can be obtained at www.ICGtesting.com
Printed in the USA
BVOW07s1239250215

389225BV00001B/391/P